Giovanna Magi

Masterpieces of the
EGYPTIAN MUSEUM
of Cairo

BONECHI

* * *

© Copyright 1997 by
CASA EDITRICE BONECHI
Via Cairoli, 18/b
FLORENCE - ITALY

Printed in Italy by
Centro Stampa Editoriale Bonechi.

Graphics: Miriam Somigli

Photographs by Gianni Dagli Orti:
pages 5, 8, 11, 15, 16, 17, 18, 19
(low), 20, 21, 22, 23, 25, 26, 27 (low),
28, 29 (above), 31, 33, 36, 37, 45, 47,
49, 51, 52, 53, 54, 55, 56, 57 (left), 58,
59, 60, 61.

Photographs by Luigi Di Giovine:
pages 3, 4, 6, 7, 9, 10, 12, 13, 14, 19
(above), 24, 27 (above), 29 (low), 32,
34, 35, 38, 39, 40, 41, 42, 43, 44, 46,
48, 50, 57 (right), 62.

ISBN 88 7009 235 6

A Brief History of the Museum

The imposing building which presently hosts the Cairo Egyptian Museum at Midan el-Tahir, was designed by the French architect, Marcel Dourgnon, winner of an international competition.

Today the Museum hosts the most important and grandiose collection of Egyptian art in the world; it has had, however, a complex and difficult past.

There has been European interest in Egyptian antiquities since the beginning of the XVIII century: the Napoleonic campaign of 1798, the discovery of the Rosetta Stone the following year and above all the publication of the 18 volume «Description de l'Egypte» between 1809 and 1816, not only gave a rigorously systematic definition to the study of Egyptian civilization but increased the appetite of those who had already begun to collect ancient objects like sarcofagi, statuettes and scarabs. There were, in fact, numerous persons living in Egypt at that time who by no means looked down upon the gifts bestowed by over generous Pashas on their guests. Amongst the first to start collecting these antiquities were the consuls of various European countries: Drovetti, the French consul and his agent Rifaud; Salt, the British consul, aided by Belzoni of Padua and Caviglia of Genoa; Giuseppe di Nizzoli from Trieste who was the Chancellor of the Austrian Legation. These collections were then sold in Europe and made up the original nucleus of Egyptian collections in various European museums such as those of Turin. Paris, London and Berlin.

The artistic and archeological heritage of Egypt thus suffered serious losses: the situation was, in fact, so serious that in 1830 a scholar of the Champollian school, asked the Pasha Mohammed Ali to set up a service to safeguard the preservation of the monuments. The former leniency seemed to have come to an end in 1834, when a Museum was founded on the banks of Lake Ezbekiah where all the objects were catalogued. These first origins were soon transferred to a more suitable site in the citadel of Cairo: there were still so few items that it was possible to fit them all into one room! The Archduke Maximilian of Austria saw these objects during a visit to Cairo in 1855 and asked the Pasha Abbas to give him some items: the Pasha gave him everything in the room and so the first original Cairo Egyptian Museum can today be seen... in Vienna!

Fortunately, on the 1st June 1858, Auguste Mariette, one of the directors of the Louvre Museum, also sent out to Egypt to collect antiquities, was able to get himself appointed «Mamour», that is Director of Excavations. The numerous pressures on Kedivé Said to preserve Egyptian monuments as well as the influential support of the general consul and important French businessmen, allowed Mariette to be granted use of the former headquarters of a river navigation company at Boulak, a small port near Cairo.

Mariette moved there with his family (he remained in Cairo for the rest of his life) and began what would become the first national museum of the whole Middle Eastern area: the official opening was on the 18th October 1863.

In 1891, the collections were moved to the Gizeh Palace and finally in 1902 to their present location.

Colossi Group of Amon-Ofis III with his wife Tiyi

The Cairo Egyptian Museum greets us in a grandiose manner with this group of colossi over ten metres high from Medinet Habu. It depicts the pharaoh Amon-Ofis III with his much loved wife Tiyi, a Syrian princess famous for her beauty, the future mother of Akhen-Aton, the heretic pharaoh. The king even had a one and a half kilometre long artificial lake constructed for her. She was so loved that, as can be seen from this group, the pharaoh had her depicted the same height as himself when traditionally the female figure was shorter than the man by a quarter. Tiyi had an increasing influence in court, especially during the last few years of Amon-Ofis III's reign.

Colossal Statue of Ramses II

This colossus comes from the present El Achmunein, the ancient Khmenu (the «city of the eight Thots»), Hermopolis for the Greeks. It is made of granite and depicts Ramses II the Great, an almost mythical figure in the secular history of Egypt, whose fame and memory has passed unblemished through time. Ramses' reign began at around about 1290 B.C. and he died at over ninety years old in 1224. He enjoyed displaying his power in the colossal monuments which have immortalized him: Abu Simbel, Luxor, Karnak.

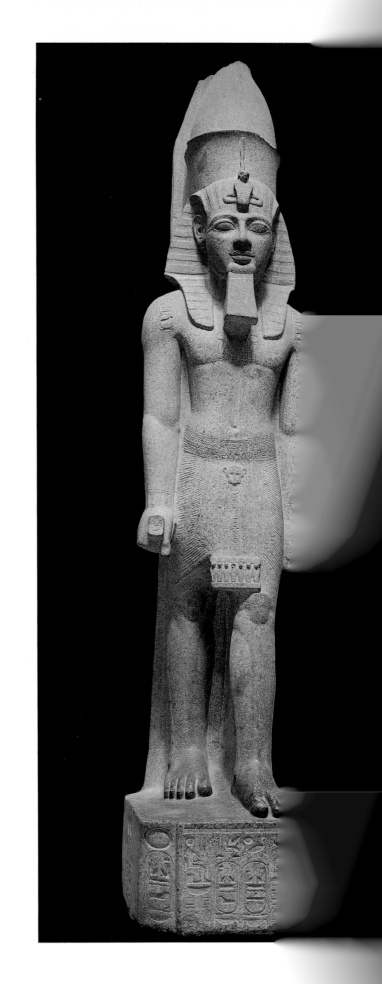

The «Narmer Stele»

This small engraved sandstone stele (74 cm high) is in fact a cosmetics tablet, with a central hollow for preparing eye cosmetics: it can be dated at around 3100 B.C. i.e. the beginning of the predynastic era. The scenes engraved on both sides in bas-relief recall one of the principal events in the history of the country, the unification of Upper and Lower Egypt during Narmer's reign. Egyptologists have discussed the identity of this king at length: it is probable that Narmer, whose name appears between two calves' heads high up on the tablet symbolized by the fish (n'r) and chisel (mr), can be identified with the legendary Menes, who Herodotus tells us was the founder of the Egyptian dynasties.

On this side the king, wearing the conical crown of Upper Egypt, with one hand grasps the hair of a prostrated enemy whose arms are open begging for mercy and with the other grips the club which will deal the finishing blow; on the above right, Horus the hawk-God is depicted bringing prisoners, symbolized by an ethnically well distinguished head. On the other side, Narmer is wearing the cap type crown of Lower Egypt. From then on the royal crown is double, made up of the union between Upper and Lower Egypt.

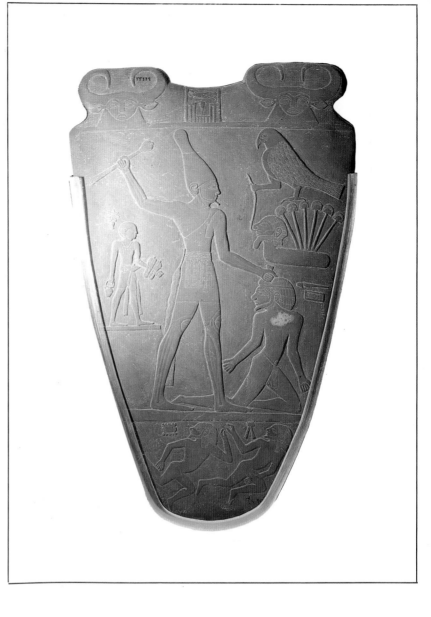

The Micerinus Triad

This famous IVth dynasty group comes from the valley temple of Micerinus who built the third Gizeh pyramid. Out of the forty-two making up the original series, only four are now intact.

Here the pharaoh is depicted advancing arrogantly from the background, beside the goddess Hathor with calf horns and solar disk and the personification of one of the 42 Egyptian provinces with the territory symbol above the head: in this case the figure on the right represents Diopolis Parva, the ancient city of Het where Hathor and Neftis were adored.

Statue of King Zoser

This 1.40 metre high limestone statue represents the great pharaoh Zoser, founder of the IIIrd dynasty. This statue comes from his tomb which is one of the most complex monuments left by Egyptian art: the «huge step» pyramid of Sakkarah is a true architectural miracle constructed by the first historically known architect, Imhotep, called «son of Ptah», who was also a doctor of such fame that two thousand years later the Greeks deified him with the name Esculapius. The statue was in the «serdab» («cellar» in arabic), a closed room inside the pyramid with slits looking onto the adjacent chambers where the funeral ceremony was held. Here were kept statues of the deceased which thus became a «substitute» for the true body. The image of the pharaoh is wrapped in the cloak the king wore for the sumptuous ceremony of «Hebsed», a celebration which confirmed the royalty of the sovereign. On his head rests the «nemes», a heavy head-dress of pleated material with a false beard on his chin. The eyes, originally inlaid, must have given a touch of liveliness to the solemn, highly expressive, richly humanitarian face.

Statue of Kefren

Sitting on his throne of black diorite, with his right hand
symbolically closed in a fist, in this
statue Kefren, the half-brother and successor
of Keope, completely fulfills the ideal of the pharaoh
who is God and man at the same time.
On the sides of the throne are sculptured
the symbols of the two countries
which united make up his kingdom: the papyrus,
symbol of Upper Egypt, and the lotus,
symbol of Lower Egypt, are intertwined
around the hieroglyphic sign
meaning «unity».
The God Horus is positioned at the back
of the king's neck in the form of a hawk,
with its wings outspread, giving protection
and advice to the king.
The hard stone used to make the statue, came
from a quarry in the Nubia
desert, over 1000 km from where this piece
was actually sculptured.

Wooden Statue of Ka-Aper

When this statue was discovered in 1860, the Egyptian excavation workmen were struck by its physical similarity to the head of their village. Thus this statue has always been linked to the playful nickname «head of the village» (Cheik El-Beled). It really depicts Ka-Aper, the «first reading priest» who lived in Memphis at around 2500 B.C. It is made of a single block of sycamore wood apart from the arms which are attached to the trunk with pieces of wood. The image is depicted in the classical position of the Egyptian nobility: fully frontal with the left leg slightly forward, the left arm raised and holding a stick, the right arm by his side tightly grasping a sceptre, since lost. The dress was simply a short skirt, knotted at the waist. The very realistic face, with protruding eyes in a different material and the care of the sculptor to rigidly observe the stylistic rules without losing sight of reality, make this one of the most refined examples of Egyptian statues.

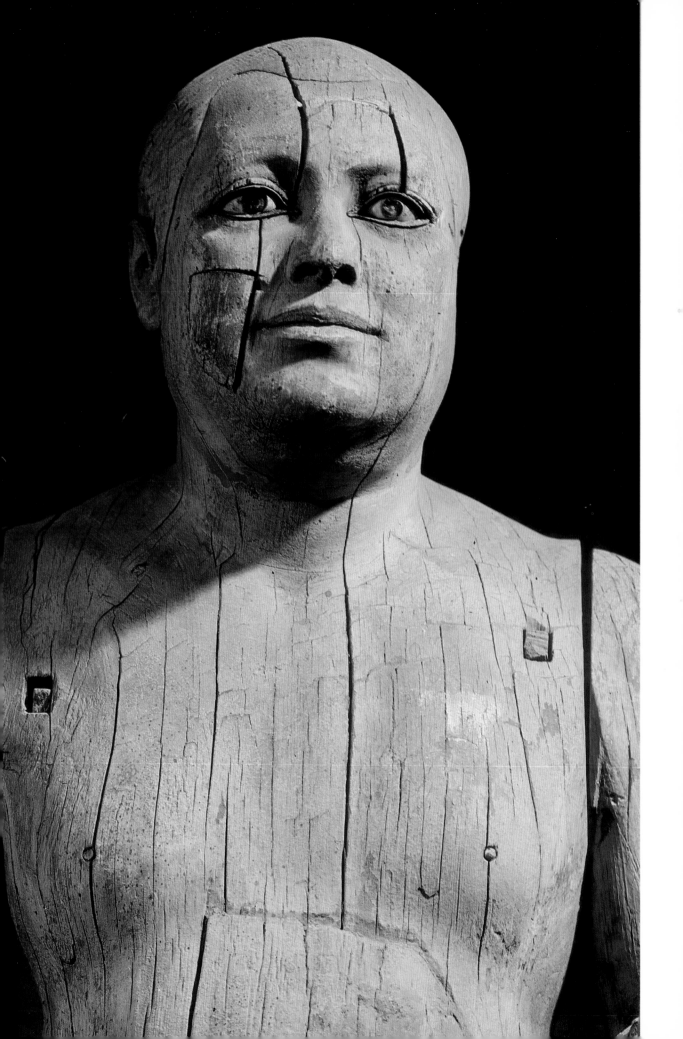

Statue of a sitting Scribe

This statuette comes from a tomb in Sakkarah and is made of painted limestone with the eyes encrusted. It was made during the period of the IVth dynasty and is the first to represent an activity. Of all the numerous professions in Ancient Egypt, that of the scribe was without doubt one of the most important, so much so that almost magical powers were attributed to writing. The scribe mainly set and collected the taxes which he himself did not have to pay. Here the scribe is depicted in the typical position, sitting cross-legged with the tablet on which the sheet of papyrus was spread.

The dwarf Seneb and his family

This apparently modest, VIth dynasty, small group of statues in painted limestone, completely revolutionizes the artistic and aesthetic rules of the period. The dwarf Seneb, head of the royal weaving whose wife could use the title of princess, is depicted here. With an unusual realism for Egyptian sculpture, the dwarf's deformity is emphasized, made even more evident next to the gentle, perfect figure of his wife. The symmetry of the composition, sharply interrupted by the man's short legs is surprisingly re-established by the unexpected inclusion of their two children. The affectionate cordiality of the wife towards her husband is to be noted, as with her hand she tenderly holds the man's short, deformed arm.

Group of Ra-Hotep and Nofret

It was the custom in Egypt for the mastabas of relations and officials to be lined up next to the royal pyramid in a precisely planned arrangement, so as to be united with their sovereign even in the last journey to the hereafter. At Mejdum, not far from the pyramid of Snefru, army general and High Priest, is the tomb of his son Ra-Hotep, who arranged for his statue to be placed next to one of his wife, Nofret.

It is said that when they were discovered in 1871, the workmen were so struck by the liveliness of their faces that they ran away in terror, thinking that they were still alive! It is in fact the almost miraculous liveliness of the faces and great stylization together with a complete respect for reality, which makes these two statues made from two separate blocks but obviously conceived together in unity, one of the highest expressions of Memphis art. Ra-Hotep with his young muscular body, has short hair and a moustache despite the Egyptian custom of shaving the hair and beard. Next to him there is Nofret «the beautiful one», with all the mystery of her beautiful body delicately wrapped and bound up in a white cloak underlining and revealing her rounded shape.

Funeral Chapel of Eika and Imerit

This wooden funeral chapel belonged to Imerit, wife of Eika and priestess of the goddess Hathor during the IVth dynasty. On the architrave and the beams supporting it are engraved numerous inscriptions in hieroglyphics with the names and titles of the owners; above the architrave there is a panel representing the deceased sitting at the funeral table.

Portrait of Hesy-Ra

Next to Zoser's pyramid at Sakkarah is the mastaba of Hesy-Ra, «Great one of the South» and «friend of the King». Inside a niche, eleven panels of sculptured wood were found depicting the deceased in various poses. Here, in best Egyptian tradition, the shoulders are rigidly forward whilst the head and the rest of the body outline the surrounding space with their profile. The space in front of him is filled with his attributes in an almost abstract way: the sceptre, quill and palette.

The Geese of Mejdum

The Geese of Mejdum may be the oldest Ancient Egyptian wall painting discovered.
It is a 1.73 metre long plaster «tempera» from the tomb of Itat at Mejdum, made at the beginning of the IVth dynasty, around 2700 B.C. The panel on display at the Museum was obviously part of a much bigger composition and it is easy to imagine the wealth and naturalistic vivacity of the work in its entirety.

The drawing is highly stylized and the colours have no shading or shadowing. The profile of the animals is clean and rigorously symmetrical. Amongst all this abstraction however, there is a colourful enjoyment and affectionate participation in reality and nature.

Head of Ra-Nofer

The gloomy features of Ra-Nofer, High Priest in Memphis around 2500 B.C., profet of Ptah and Sokaris, are the most striking elements of this beautiful painted limestone statue, 1.80 metres high, which comes from Sakkarah. In this statue, characterized by an extreme simplicity, with the light caressing and modelling the surface, the noble head particularly captures our attention: the deeply hollowed out plaited wig (which Egyptian dignitaries often wore during ceremonies) frames the face, emphasizing it in contrast with the dark dorsal slab.

Hesy-Ra at Table

Another «snap» of Hesy-Ra on the third panel from the tomb chamber. Here the deceased is sitting at a sumptuously laid table so that his spirit (according to Egyptian beliefs) could be nourished and continue to survive. Even now he does not leave the attributes of his rank behind: with his left hand he holds the sceptre and stick of command and on his right shoulder rest some writing materials.

19

Copper Statue of Pepi I

Truly unique amongst all the sculptures of the Old Kingdom, this statue represents the pharaoh Pepi I of the VIth dynasty, a period in which art reached exceedingly high levels. Given the intrinsic value and perishable nature of the material, this statue of Pepi I is the only metal statue of these dimensions discovered to this day. The statue was made by moulding embossed copper plates fixed to the centre of the wood with copper nails. The face seems to have been casted and the eyes mounted with precious materials.

False-door of Iteti

In Old Kingdom mastabas it is fairly typical to find a false-door stele in wood or limestone from which the deceased appeared with his own image to participate in the ceremonies and funeral banquets carried out in his honour in the various internal chambers of the mastaba. The outline of the chapel was always the same: on top, the deceased was depicted sitting at the table, on the architrave and at the sides the list of offerings was written in hieroglyphics and in the central niche, a high relief statue of the deceased was sculptured to maintain communication with the living. This large funeral chapel (2.20 metres wide and 3.40 metres high) comes from the mastaba of Iteti, an official who lived between the end of the Vth and the beginning of the VIth dynasty: he was «Head of the Ten of Upper Egypt» and «transport inspector».

Statue of Sesostri I

This small, 57 cm high statuette in painted cedarwood, depicts the pharaoh Sesostri I. It comes from a tomb near the king's pyramid at Licht, a small village between Cairo and El Fayyum on the edge of the desert near the probable location of Amon Emhat I's capital. Sesostri I was the son and successor of Amon Emhat I and continued his father's policies in Nubia, reaching the third cataract and seizing the gold mines of Wadi Allaki. To avoid further danger of the internal plots which had led to the assassination of his father, Sesostri became the first pharaoh in history to associate his eldest son with the throne and all his successors followed his example. In this statuette, characterized by a natural abandonment of the limbs in respect to the trunk, the pharaoh is wearing the conical crown of Upper Egypt: at the Metropolitan Museum of New York, there is a statuette of similar proportions and pose wearing the crown of Lower Egypt which is probably the «companion» to this one.

Statue of Montu-Hotep I

Completely different from the previous statue,
this depicts the pharaoh Montu-Hotep I and was made from grey
painted sandstone: it comes
from the extraordinary funerary complex of the
temple of Montu-Hotep I at Deir el-Bahari, which leant against
the rocky mountain wall dominating it. The period was the
XIth dynasty, which brought an end to the long
and troubled «first interim period»,
shaken by domestic struggles and social upheaval.
The reign of Montu-Hotep I was a long and happy one:
the pharaoh re-established power over Lower Egypt with
the support of the Egyptian bourgeoise
and got rid of the dangerous «nomarchs» who had previously
taken over power.
This coarse, at first sight almost medieval statue,
is striking because of its violent
and elementary colouring.
The almost perfect state in which it has been preserved
could be due to its peculiar destiny:
wrapped in bandages like a mummy,
it was buried in a hollow made in the rock
as though it were to substitute the king's corpse.
The statue, wearing a short dress
was part of a group of eight statues,
probably in the same position,
located in a vast clearing in front of the temple
in the shade of the trees.

Cubic Statue of Senmut with the Princess Neferu-Ra

Egyptian art has always had the tendency of having extremely stylized and geometrized forms: this is evident in the so-called cubic statues, the first examples of which come from the Middle Kingdom.

This statue in black granite, 1.40 m high, comes from Karnak. It belongs to the XVIIIth dynasty and depicts a famous character in Egyptian history, Senmut, minister and architect of Queen Hatshepsut and tutor of her daughter, the Princess Neferu-Ra. His rôle as tutor was so important that Senmut often had himself portrayed with the princess on his knee or in his arms. In this example, the body of the character seems to be imprisoned in one mass: the dress, thickly covered in hieroglyphics, covers the whole block of granite, from which emerges the domineering head of the teacher and that of his pupil. They both appear to be united by a sort of affectionate complicity.

Head of Sesostri III

This head, made of black granite, 29 cm high, comes from Medamud, a village near Thebes which had a temple dedicated to the God Montu, restored and enlarged by Sesostri III. It is thus almost certain that this head can be attributed to Sesostri III, not only due to its origin but also because of the physical features of the face, thanks to the special talent for portrayal which has always marked Egyptian statues.

Sesostri III, one of the most important Egyptian pharaohs, continued the work of his predecessors consolidating the colonization of Nubia and building a series of fortresses along the border, connected by a system of smoke signals.

Statue of Sesostri I

This beautiful, 1.90 metre high statue in Tura limestone, is one of a group of ten similarly made statues of the same dimensions, found lying on the ground in a large courtyard next to the king's pyramid at Licht. The frontal pose of the pharaoh expresses all the solemnity and regality of his office.

Head of Nefertiti

It is difficult to talk about this excellent example of Amarnian art, apart from the physical beauty of the face. This splendid head, made from quartzite, was never finished — in fact, on the forehead, nose and eyes, it is still possible to see the guide line for a further colour which was never applied. It depicts Nefertiti, princess of the Mitans, wife-sister of Akhen-Aton, who played an important rôle in the arts and customs revolution of her husband. It is in fact its incompleteness which gives a touch of mystery to the melancholic beauty of the queen, whose name means «the beautiful one who comes here», with her soft mouth, languid eyes and slender neck which bears the purest profile. It even seems that the sculptor (possibly a certain Tutmose whose workshop has come to light at Tell el-Amarna) managed to penetrate the psychology of the queen and interpret her most hidden emotions which seem to vibrate in the surprisingly mobile expression of her beautiful face.

Domestic Altar with the family of Akhen-Aton

This limestone tablet from Tell el-Amarna, depicts the pharaoh Akhen-Aton with his wife and children: above them shines the solar disk of Aton with the ureus. The disk emits rays which end in the «ankh», the symbol of life which the supreme God bestows on mortals.

Head of a Princess Daughter of Akhen-Aton

This small, seven centimetre high head, made of red quartzite, is related to other heads depicting the princess daughters of Akhen-Aton. In fact, the outstanding somatic features of the head resemble him: the irregular development, pointed chin, swollen mouth and protruding ears. Here again the constant search for realism which characterizes Amarnian art can be seen.

Fresco from the Tomb of Nefertari

The tomb of Nefertari, favourite wife of Ramses II, is without doubt the most beautiful tomb of the whole Theban necropolis known as «the Valley of the Queens». Unfortunately, today it is still closed due to the serious influx of water which threatens the frescoes. The royal tomb is entirely painted with mythical characters and sacred animals although there is also an «irreverent» type of painting in which the queen, richly attired, is depicted playing chess. This painting was on the first wall of the first chamber of Nefertari's tomb, discovered in 1904 by an Italian archeological expedition led by Ernesto Schiaparelli.

Architectural Colossus of Akhen-Aton

Around the end of the XVIIIth dynasty, there was a profound transformation in Egypt, mainly of a religious nature. The young pharaoh Amon-Ofis IV, frightened by the clergy of Amon who had almost created a state within a state, substituted the worship of Amon for that of Aton, the solar disk. This new cult did not require the use of images so he closed the temples, dispersed the priests and abandoned Thebes for a new capital Akhet-Aton («the horizon of Aton», now called Tell el-Amarna). His final act was to change his own name from Amon-Ofis, which means «Amon is pleased», to Akhen-Aton, which means «this pleases Aton». The new religious creed also had repercussions in the art world which no longer pursued a purely exterior beauty and returned to more simple and intimate ideals, concentrating on the physical features of the subject depicted. Pictorial art was very much helped in this by the physical formation of the pharaoh: a long series of incestuous marriages perhaps resulted in the particular appearance portrayed by Aken-Aton in his statues. The swollen and protruding stomach, the wide hips, fleshy lips, oblong head and large ears make up a series of physical defects which are underlined with extraordinary realism in this series of architectural colossi in sandstone which the «heretic pharaoh» wished to be erected in the temple of Karnak.

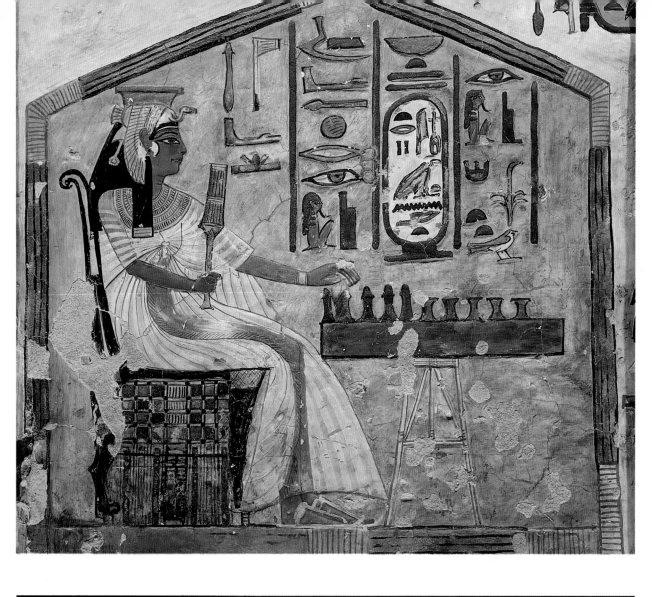

Papyrus of the « Book of the Dead »

At the Cairo Egyptian Museum there are numerous examples of papyri: the majority of these are copies of the *Book of the Dead*, a basic collection of prayers and magical-religious formulas superbly illustrated, which were placed inside the tombs from around 1600 B.C. onwards. With these texts, the deceased could safely face the long journey to the Elysian Fields, assured of the protection of the Gods in the hereafter.

TREASURES OF TUTANKHAMON
Story of a discovery

The discovery of Tutankhamon's tomb is one of the most fascinating chapters in the history of archeology. As well as the fairy-tale nature of the discovery, the amazing wealth of artistic heritage found should be remembered.

Even if only briefly, this story deserves to be told.

In 1922, the Englishman Lord Carnarvon, art collector and globe trotter, had already invested around £ 50.000 to finance various excavation expeditions in Egypt with no results. His great hope of finding something magnificent, maybe even the intact tomb of a pharaoh, was fading. His missions were directed by another Englishman, Howard Carter, who had studied in Egypt with the famous archeologist Petrie, and had a particular preference for the mass of rocky ravines and inaccessible gorges around Thebes called «the Valley of the Kings». At that time the whole valley had been explored and it was commonly agreed that there was no trace at all of only three sovereigns of the XVIIIth dynasty: Akhen-Aton, Tutankhamon, and Horemheb. For the first and last of these three, there was no hope at all: the heretic king almost certainly did not have an official burial and the final resting place of the general was elsewhere. That left Tutankhamon, the transition pharaoh, who returned the capital to Thebes, restoring the ancient cult of Amon-Ra and other Gods, even changing his own name from Tut-Ankh-Aton to Tut-Ankh-Amon. His reign was very short, barely nine years, and he died young (nearly nineteen years old) around about 1350 B.C. So Lord Carnarvon decided that this would be his last mission in Egypt. The big discovery came on the 4th November 1922: almost at the base of the tomb of Ramses VI, a stone step came to light which led to a second and then a third descending until sixteen steps were freed, which came to an end in front of a sealed door, walled up with mortar.

Thus began one of the most wonderful human and scientific adventures in history.

Carter covered over the steps and rushed to telegraph the news of the discovery to Carnarvon who set off for Egypt straight away with his daughter Evelyn. As it later transpired, even this tomb had been broken into several times by robbers and pillagers: but to what extent? And above all: would they find the mummy intact?

The 26th November was the «day of all days» for Carter: after breaking down a second door with the seals of the boy-pharaoh still intact, the Englishman made a small opening with an iron bar which he then passed through the hole meeting no obstacle. He did a test with a match, finding no traces of gas. Finally, by candlelight he put his head against the gap and as his eyes slowly became accustomed to the darkness, «strange animals, statues and gold, slowly emerged from the dark, gold glittered everywhere...». «Wonderful things!» exclaimed Carter, his voice broken with emotion, to the impatient Lord Carnarvon behind him asking what he could see.

The wonderful things were the imposing funerary furnishings described later on. This was only the beginning. First, however, long months went by full of quarrels with the Egyptian authorities and tragic events (the sudden death of Lord Carnarvon) as well as the difficult and painstaking work of restoring the sensational furnishings which Carter then sent on bit by bit to the Cairo Museum. Of all the precious objects in the sovereign's tomb, the discovery of the great sarcophagus made the biggest impression: it is a single, enormous block of quartzite enclosed in four gilded wooden cases, fitting into each other like Russian dolls and only after all of them had been dismantled (84 days of exhausting work to bring the 80 pieces constituting the four catafalques up to the light of the valley) could Carter admire the brilliant colours of the paintings adorning the walls of the burial chamber. The sarcophagus is of an exceptional beauty, «worthy of holding the mortal remains of a king».

On the 12th February 1924 in the presence of nineteen illustrious guests, a complex winch raised the

Valley of the Kings - Tutankhamon's tomb: the first sarcophagus.

The famous funeral mask of Tutankhamon, in gold and semi-precious stones, reproduces almost exactly the delicate features of the pharaoh. This was placed over the king's head and shoulders. On the back an inscription in hieroglyphics identifies the various parts of the king's face with those of the main Egyptian gods.

one and a half tonnes of granite which made up the lid of the sarcophagus. When Carter directed the light of his lamp inside, his first view must have been a bitter disappointment: there were only some discoloured linen cloths! However, once these were slowly removed, at last appeared the king... and the gold: a wooden, sarcophagus entirely covered in gold foil and inlaid with glass and semi-precious stones with the pharaoh representing Osiris, his face in an amazing expression of serenity and severity. However, tells Carter, in all that flare the most moving thing was a small wreath of flowers, perhaps a last gesture to the deceased pharaoh from his young consort Ankhesenamen: those humble dried up flowers, thirty-two centuries later, have still preserved some of their original colouring.

At this stage of Carter's works and discoveries, there was a long pause during which the English archeologist left Egypt amid misunderstandings and disputes with the Egyptian authorities, for a long conference tour of America. Almost a year later, on the 25th January 1925, Carter was back at the king's sarcophagus for the latest exciting adventures. The lid of the *first anthropoidal sarcophagus* (2.25 metres long) was also raised: inside there were more linen bandages adorned with garlands of flowers (in fact, examination of the wreaths of flowers helped to establish the season in which the sovereign was buried. This was probably between the end of March and the beginning of April, because botanists recognize lilies amongst the flowers, which are in fact gathered during that period).

Under the sheet was a *second anthropoidal sarcophagus*, a little more than two metres long: this was also in gilded wood, encrusted with pieces of coloured glass and semi-precious stones. Eight men were needed to raise the lid of this second coffin: at this stage Carter may have been expecting to find a *third sarcophagus*, he certainly did not expect to see what appeared before his astonished eyes in the powerful lamplight. The third cof-

To the side and above, two details of the third huge gold sarcophagus; on the cover of the sarcophagus, the goddesses Neftis and Isis bring the dead pharaoh back to life, whilst the other two gods Nekhbet and Uadjet, carved in cloisonné, open their wings to protect the mummy. The pharaoh's false beard is a divine symbol, as are the attributes which the king holds in his hands, the whip and the sceptre, symbols of the two reigns of Upper and Lower Egypt.

fin, 1.85 metres long, was a massive block of 22 carat gold, weighing about 1.170 kilos! «An incredible mass of pure gold»: its material value alone was priceless! In addition to the headgear with a cobra and vulture, the king wore a false beard and a heavy necklace of gold and majolic beads, whilst in his hands he held the whip and the sceptre, symbols of the two Egyptian kingdoms; the Gods Nekhbet and Buto spread out their wings to protect the mummy, and Neftis and Isis bring the dead pharaoh back to life.

It is easy to imagine the emotion and reverential awe experienced by Carter as he approached the contents of this last coffin, which he knew contained the mummy of Tutankhamon. The mummy was in fact completely covered in jewels and gold.

Again the delicate, serene features of the nineteen year old king could be seen on the shining *gold mask* with a covering of semi-precious stones to the shoulders: particularly elegant is the heavy blue and gold striped «nemes» with royal symbols on the forehead, inlaid with lapislazuli, turquoises and cornelians.

On the whole of the king's mummy (unfortunately in a disastrous condition), Carter counted over 143 precious objects including rings, breast plates, bracelets and girdles.

Three sarcophagi, four funerary cases, kilos of gold had protected the humble remains of the great Tutankhamon from mortal eyes for 132 centuries.

Breastplate with solar and lunar emblems

This breastplate is one of the most beautiful jewels of the whole Tutankhamon treasure and because of the complexity of its various parts and their meaning, it deserves to be described with care. The central part of the jewel is made up of a chalcedony scarab which at the same time forms the body of a hawk with its wings spread out: this is pushing a boat with the eye *udjat* in the centre and at the side, two elegantly wound papyrus flowers support two urei, surmounted by the solar disk. The central eye, i.e. Horus' left eye, sustains a silver crescent moon and full moon which represent Thot and Horus who protect Tutankhamon who is now also a God. At the back, the scarab holds a lily in its left claw and a lotus in the right claw, the symbols of Upper and Lower Egypt. At the sides of the two flowers, there are two urei and under a band of circles there is a series of pendants in the form of flower buds.

Flabellum for Ceremonial Fan

This flabellum comes from the funeral chamber of the young king, symbolically in the shade, and is placed at the end of a 94 cm long gold handle ending in the form of a stylized lotus flower. It was used to support the hugh ostrich feather fans for processions and religious ceremonies. It is made of wood, covered in gold leaf and engraved with scenes of ostrich hunting. As can be read from an inscription, the fan was made from « ostrich feathers procured by the king during a hunting beat in the desert to the east of Heliopolis ».

Detail of the gold mask of Tutankhamon.

Treasures of Tutankhamon

Earring   *Treasures of Tutankhamon*

Breastplate in the form of a Scarab

This simple and highly elegant breastplate was made of gold, inlaid with pieces of lapislazuli, cornelians, turquoises and green feldspars. It represents a winged scarab which sustains the solar disk. The good supply of precious and semi-precious stones in Egypt encouraged the artisans to liberally use them in the creation of these jewels.

There were turquoise mines (the stone dedicated to Hathor) in the Sinai and the green feldspar and cornelians came from the eastern Egyptian desert, whereas the lapislazuli were imported from Afghanistan.

The same materials used for the breastplate also make up this beautiful earring which was perhaps made to commemorate Tutankhamon's coronation celebrations. The young king is in fact depicted in the centre of the ring, flanked by two urei holding the solar disk. Underneath the ring there are six rows of beads which end in drops of gold and coloured glass.

On the left, a view of the whole gilded wood chapel, with the goddesses Isis and Selkhet who protect the canopic jars inside. On the right, a detail of the goddess Isis, with the eyes and eyebrows heavily accentuated in black.

Treasures of Tutankhamon

«Canopic Naos»

«...I am not ashamed to say that I was not able to utter a single word»: thus wrote Howard Carter remembering the moment he discovered this large coffer, called the «canopic naos» because it was used to hold the canopic jars of the pharaoh. His emotion and astonishment must have been very great indeed because this naos is one of the most beautiful and most important pieces of the Tutankhamon treasure. It is a large gilded wooden case, with the hieroglyphic inscriptions surmounted by a row of urei sustaining the solar disk. On the four sides of the case lean four female statuettes, wearing long, finely pleated dresses, with their heads slightly turned and their arms open in a silently graceful movement and a gently protective posture. They are the four goddesses which protect the four canopic jars inside: Isis protectress of the liver, Selkhet of the intestines, Neftis of the lungs and Neith of the stomach. There is a scorpion on the head of the statue of Selkhet, which is the Egyptian symbol of resurrection.

On the page opposite, a detail of the decoration on a wall of the little shrine with the queen bathing the pharaoh's body in ointments.

Treasures of Tutankhamon

Small Gold Naos (called the naos of the royal statues)

This is a small sanctuary with a wooden double door also completely covered in gold and resting on silver covered supports with ebony latches. It is modelled on the sanctuary of Nekhbet, the goddess vulture of Upper Egypt. It was called the «naos of the royal statues» because when it was dis-covered it was, unfortunately, empty except for the pedestal which revealed the former presence of a statue, or rather two statues. The coffer no doubt contained a pair of statues of the king and queen, stolen when the tomb was broken into by the first grave robbers. The decoration is truly beautiful: the vulture of the goddess Nekhbet is depicted 14 times on the roof together with the sign «shen» meaning eternity and cartouches with the royal names. On the walls, the decoration represents the king and queen in intimate and affectionate poses, such as the one in which the young woman, sumptuously dressed in linen, anoints Tutankhamon. Here Tutankhamon wears the blue crown or *khepresh* whilst behind him flies the vulture bringing the sign of life.

41

Funeral Bed Head

When Carter entered the Antechamber of the royal tomb on the 26th November 1922, he found the most incredible collection of funeral furnishings he had ever seen: three huge beds made in the form of animals astonishingly loaded with vases, precious objects, caskets, statues and statuettes, dominated the narrow room. The sides of one bed are in the form of a lioness, another is made up of animals which are half hippopotamus and half crocodile; the third bed, by far the most beautiful, has sides made of slender bodied cows with very elegant lyre-shaped horns on their heads enclosing the solar disk to symbolize the sacred cow of the goddess Hathor. These beds almost certainly had a magical function as the imaginary vehicle for the pharaoh's last journey. It is, however, possible that they were used when installing the king in the tomb.

Golden Statuettes of the Pharaoh

As with all the other gilded wood statuettes in this group, these were also completely covered, except for the faces, in pieces of linen with the date they were woven written in ink. The statuette on the left is a magnificent piece of sculpture because the subject is realistically depicted carrying out an action, which is rare for Egyptian modelling. The pharaoh, standing on a fragile papyrus barge, is about to throw a harpoon: this represents the God Horus who is about to harpoon Set transformed, according to the legend, into a hippopotamus. The king is wearing the red crown of Lower Egypt whilst in the statuette on the right he is holding a curved stick and whip and wearing the white symbol of Upper Egypt.

Golden Throne

The animal theme which characterizes the majority of Tutankhamon's
funeral furnishings is also to be found in this splendid wooden throne
entirely covered in gold and mounted with semi-precious stones and
glass paste. At the sides of the seat there are in fact two superb lion
heads which represent the two horizons, east and west; the chairlegs,
solidly placed on the cylindrical bases, are in the form of lion paws; the
armrests are two serpents with their wings outspread, embracing and
protecting the cartouche with the pharaoh's name.
Particularly striking is the intimate and homely scene on the back of the
throne, very much in contrast to all the splendour and regal solemnity:
the king's gentle consort, Ankhesenamen, tenderly reaches out her arms
to anoint her husband with unguents, whilst the sun above beams
life-giving rays down on the royal couple.
In all this glitter of gold, the couple is dressed in silver with the exposed
parts in red glass and wide collars representing flower necklaces are
inlaid with coloured glass and cornelians.

On the right, the splendid decoration
the back of the golden throne, portray
the royal couple.

The Small «Hunting» Coffer

This is a wooden coffer decorated with gouache painting on plaster. Both sides are painted with battle scenes in which Tutankhamon, standing upright on his chariot, attacks and defeats hordes of Asian and African enemies. This is, naturally, an imaginary battle because it is highly improbable that the barely adolescent king participated in any wars. It is more a symbolic representation of his power, as is indicated by the fact that the king occupies the whole central part of the scene, dominating everything else depicted in much smaller dimensions.

Ceremonial Throne

This throne, quite different in its conception and style from the golden throne, is a highly refined example of craft-work with elegant proportions and colouring. It is sometimes called «ecclesiastic», a prototype of the episcopal throne (pulpit) in the Christian Church. The back is encrusted with ivory and semi-precious stones and at the top the hawk-God Horus is depicted with his wings outspread; on the top edge there is a row of urei with the solar disk in the middle. On the seat are encrustations resembling the spotted skin of the leopard; the crossed legs end in the form of a duck's head and are joined at the front by very elegant wooden fretwork representing the papyrus and lotus linked together, once again symbolizing the union of Upper and Lower Egypt.

Alabaster Canopic Jar Stopper

The four sarcophagi bearing the embalmed viscera of the pharaoh were enclosed in a splendid alabaster container divided into four compartments, each one corresponding to an organ and placed under the protection of a God. The stopper of each compartment was a head, reproducing the pharaoh's features, also made of the transparent alabaster which came from Hatnub, around 300 km from Memphis. The gentle boyish face of the pharaoh still bears traces of painting: a heavy black outline on the eyes and eyebrows, a thin line to indicate the folds of the neck and a vivid red to underline the soft lips. On the forehead the pharaoh again bears the symbols of royalty.

Canopic Sarcophagus

Reproduced here is one of the four miniature sarcophagi containing the king's viscera, which faithfully copies the form of the second anthropoidal sarcophagus of Tutankhamon. The inside of the small, precious container of the royal organs, (this one was maybe for the lungs) was lined with gold leaf completely covered in hieroglyphic inscriptions. The outside is made of gold, inlaid with cornelians and semi-precious stones. The pharaoh is depicted wearing the «nemes» head-dress with a cobra and vulture and holding the sceptre and whip.

The God Anubis

Found in the opening between the room containing the golden throne and the treasure room, covered by a pall with necklaces of flowers around the neck, the God Anubis, protector of the necropolis and in charge of mummification, is vigilantly lying down on a gold sedan-chair in the form of a pillar. The statue of the jackal-God is in wood painted with black plaster: the ears, eyes and collar are covered in gold.

The Royal « Ka » of Tutankhamon

When Carter entered the Antechamber of the pharaoh's tomb, he found «sentries» guarding the funeral chamber, in the form of two almost identical statues, armed with clubs and sticks with the left leg forward in the typical position of Egyptian nobility statues.
These represent the pharaoh's «Ka» or «double», which separates from the body at the moment of death to follow him into the hereafter. One of the two statues depicts Tutankhamon and not only reproduces his features but also his height, because compared with the mummy, it corresponds exactly to the king's real height, around 1.70 metres. The contrast between the black of the body and the young king's golden attire is beautiful and very impressive.

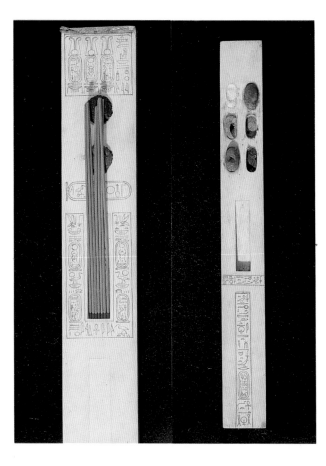

Ivory and Gold Palette   *Treasures of Tutankhamon*

The palette on the left, with the upper part in ivory and gold, is equipped with seven «reed pens» and carries an inscription in hieroglyphics with Tutankhamon's cartouche and the sentence «beloved by the Gods Aton, Amon-Ra and Thot». The palette on the right is also in ivory and has six small spaces containing traces of colour pigments. Since the scribes only wrote in red and black ink, this palette was probably also used for painting. It belonged to Merit-Amon, the eldest daughter of Akhen-Aton and Nefertiti and sister of Ankhesenamen, Tutankhamon's wife. Merit-Amon's husband, Semenkhare, co-ruled with Akhen-Aton and upon the almost simultaneous death of them both, the second son-in-law, Tutankhamon, took over the rule of Egypt.

Hawk Head

This head found in 1897 by the Egyptologist, Quibell, in the temple of Hierancopolis, where the hawk-God Horus was worshipped, is one of the most perfect examples of goldsmith art of the Memphis era. The copper body of the animal has unfortunately been lost. All that remains is this superb head made of a sheet of hammered and polished off gold, with obsidian eyes. On the head of the animal are two stylized feathers and the royal cobra. Due to its brilliance and splendour, gold was often considered by the Egyptians to be a divine material to be used in the decoration of statues of kings and Gods.

51

Mummy of Ramses II

It should be stated first of all, that the tomb of Ramses II was found completely empty: nothing is left of the enormous wealth it almost certainly contained. When the great pharaoh's mummy came to light after a long series of sackings and night time robberies, it was taken to the Cairo Egyptian Museum. Sir Gaston Maspero, Professor of the Collège de France who was the first to study the mummy upon its discovery, describes it as having a wide thorax and square shoulders with the arms crossed on the breast. The head was long and small in comparison to the 1.73 metre high body. The nose was long, slender and hooked, the round ears were pierced and the mouth small with thick lips. It seems that all his life Ramses shaved off his beard and moustache but probably let them grow during his final illness. It was also noticed that during the mummification, the pharaoh's hair was dyed with henna. In 1976, on the occasion of the big Ramses II exhibition in Paris, numerous examinations were carried out on the mummy which revealed that the pharaoh died at around 90 years old and suffered from toothache and a serious form of arthrosis of the spine. Pathetic human details about one of the greatest figures in history!

Small Female Head

This tiny head (8.50 cm high) is one of the most significant examples of Middle Kingdom art, around the beginning of the XIIth dynasty. It comes from a tomb near the pyramid of Sesostri I, at Licht, and is made of wood. The eyes must have been encrusted and the wooden wig which was added, is painted black and coated with gold. Other examples of this period confirm that these wigs were mobile and it was thus possible to change the hairstyle of the statue.

Life Scenes

On the 17th March 1920 at Deir el-Bahari, the tomb was discovered of a certain Meket-Ra «Great Superintendant and Governor of the Six Great Tribunals» who lived around 2000 B.C. The American H.E. Winlock, who discovered the tomb, found no golden funeral objects but instead 24 wooden models depicting scenes of daily life which this important official wished to be buried with him as they represented what he possessed during his life.

It is as if time has stopped on an ordinary day in the life of an ordinary rich landowner of the Middle Kingdom. Just look at the scene of the *counting of the livestock*, a common event on all Ancient Egyptian land properties. The owner is sitting under a porch with four scribes beside him. In front of him, nineteen heads of cattle of different sizes, file past led by slaves. In front of the porch, a servant is beating another slave with a stick. Other scenes include *the carpenter's shop* and *the weaver's shop*.

Models of Soldiers *(next page)*

These two groups of forty soldiers each are the only examples of their kind and come from a tomb in Assiut: the first group is armed with long bronze-tipped pikes and shields whilst the second darkskinned goup has bows and arrows. Both groups march in groups of four with the left leg forward and solidly placed on the ground. These little models in painted wood are also part of the series of characters depicted carrying out their normal activities, which make up the funeral furnishings of Middle Kingdom tombs.

55

Woman Making Beer

In Vth dynasty tombs, tiny descriptions of people carrying out various artisanal activities can often be found. Beermaking was quite laborious work, especially for women: barley seeds were crushed in a mortar, then ground and made into flour; this was then kneaded and lightly cooked in round loaves which were pounded in jars of water. A pulp was thus obtained which was filtered into vats with spouts from which the liquid was poured out, leaving the yeast on the top and the sediment below. The beer was kept in jugs: it was quite a pleasant drink and lasted for a long time before going sour.

Bearer of Offerings

This statuette in plastered painted wood, comes from Deir el-Bahari and depicts a woman elegantly and unaffectedly carrying a basket containing four pointed loaves of bread. It is interesting here to note the female clothing of the XIth dynasty. The woman is wearing a long, tight, white tunic, covered in netting maybe made of multicoloured leather. This is held up by two long shoulder straps, like braces, gathered at the breast, making this dress an ancient ancestor of the «pinafore dress» which is still often worn today.

Group of Sen-Nufer with his Wife and Daughter

This beautiful group in dark stone which comes from Karnak, dated at around 1410 B.C., depicts quite an important family of the New Kingdom. The important dignitary depicted is in fact Sen-Nufer, «Prince of the City of the South» at the time of Amon-Ofis II. He administrated the «granaries and herds» of Amon. His wife, Seth-Nofer was the «royal wetnurse» and his daughter Muthai who finishes off the group in a perfect play of balance and symmetry, was called the «singer of Amon».

Sphinx-Head of Amon-Emhat III

After many military campaigns, the XIIth dynasty ended with the exploitation of a part of the country known as Fayyum, an oasis near which the most beautiful residences of the pharaohs were built. Amon-Emhat III's residence at Hawara was so grandiose and complex that it greatly inspired the imagination of Greek travellers who referred to it as the «Labyrinth». Of all the many portraits of this pharaoh, the four which come from Tanis known as the «Tanis sphinxes» are probably the most famous. In this group, in fact, the human face of the king is not framed by the royal headdress but by a powerful lion's mane. When they were discovered, this detail caused the four sphinxes to be called the «Hyksos Monuments» due to the barbaric appearance of the heads as well as the fact that they came from Tanis — at that time the capital of the Hyksos invasion.

Statue of Thutmose III

This statue in black granite comes from Karnak and is characterized by a head with delicate features enclosed between the solid crown and the heavy false beard. It depicts one of the most famous Egyptian pharaohs who took his country to the limits of its power and glory. Thutmose III ruled for 34 years and his reign signalled the triumph of the great Egyptian empire over all the world as known at that time. In over 17 campaigns in Asia (some simply punitive but others true and proper military expeditions), Thutmose III defeated the Mitans conclusively. His victories were famous: at Kadesh, Megiddo, Karkhemish and then across the river Euphrates to beat the Mitans on their own territory, following them as far as the mountains. The Egyptian empire now even included the «islands of the big circle» — the Cyclades, Crete and Cyprus which still maintain the customs and religion. Towards the end of his reign, around 1450 B.C., Thutmose III reached the fourth cataract, bringing the borders of Egypt from Napata in Nubia (now called Gebel Barkal) to the river Euphrates.

Group of Thutmose IV with his mother Ti-O

This group in black granite which comes from Karnak has a peculiarity: the pharaoh Thutmose IV is depicted in an official statue with his mother Ti-O and not his wife. It is possible that when this statue was made the pharaoh was not yet married and so, after him, his mother was the highest person in the land. The woman is wearing the heavy so-called «vulture» hairstyle, the symbol of her royal motherhood, whilst the pharaoh has a curious almost spherical wig. The strong but affectionate crossing of the arms at the bottom of the group should be noted as well as the solid positioning in the space of the two characters who, with their vague hint of a smile and small, tight eyes, give an air of mystery.

60

Statue of the Goddess Thueris

The monstruous figure of the hippopotamus-Goddess Thueris or Ta-Urt, which means «the big one», was well-loved by the Egyptians. She joined the Egyptian pantheon relatively late, during the New Kingdom, and the cult probably originates from the regions of the Upper Nile. She has the head and body of a hippopotamus and the back of a crocodile. She is the protectress of mothers and children, in charge of breastfeeding and is always depicted upright on her hind legs with a hand placed on the hieroglyphic sign of «sa» meaning protection.

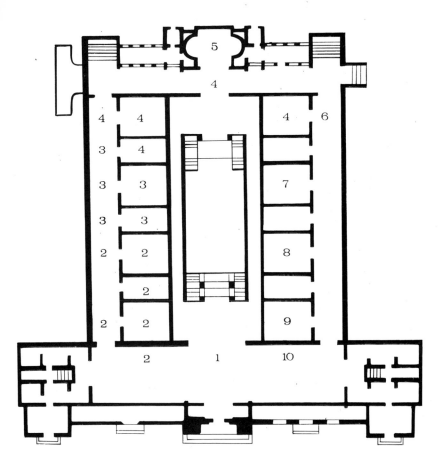

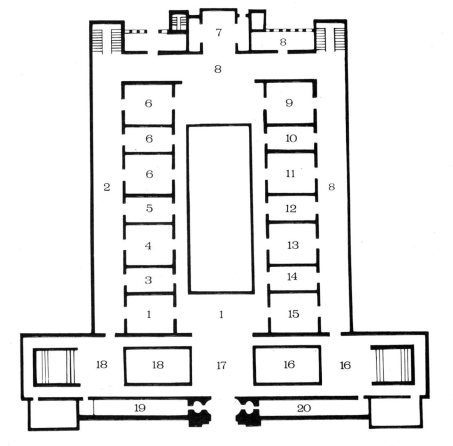

INDEX